BEYOND THE BREAKING POINT

10 CODES TO LEAD FROM CHAOS TO CLARITY

RIMANA DOLLIE K

Clever Fox® PUBLISHING

Chennai • Bangalore

CLEVER FOX PUBLISHING
Chennai, India

Published by CLEVER FOX PUBLISHING 2025

ISBN: 978-93-7500-600-8

CONTENTS

PREFACE

I have always believed that a life grounded in values is not just a personal virtue — it's a social responsibility. When we choose to live with honesty, kindness, empathy, and integrity, we do not just become better people. We create an environment where others feel safe to be themselves, too.

This book is dedicated to my beloved uncle (Jethu) Bangshi Saikia, who passed away on 24 February, 2019, but whose presence still lives on in everything I do. I remember his voice as if it were yesterday. He was steady, kind, honest — the person everyone in the family turned to. He did not teach values through speeches or through lectures. He lived them.

Through small, consistent acts of compassion — a word of advice, a listening ear, a reassuring presence — he showed us what quiet strength really looks like. He reminded us that when you take care of your inner principles, everything else falls into place: your relationships, your family, your ability to show up in the world.

That is the spirit behind this book.

In a world that often praises performance over principle, I want to offer a return — a return to the kind of clarity that comes from knowing who you are and what you stand for. The kind of strength that does not come from control or loudness, but from a deep inner alignment.

This book invites you to examine how values shape not just your choices, but your relationships, your healing, and your personal peace. When you lead with empathy, honesty, and respect, something remarkable happens: you begin to trust yourself. And when you trust yourself, you begin to understand others — not as threats, but as fellow travellers trying to make sense of their own chaos.

That is where connection begins. That is where clarity starts.

Inside these pages, you will find practical reflections, real-life stories, and simple but powerful codes to help you live more consciously and meaningfully. This is not about becoming perfect. It is about becoming real.

I hope this book helps you return to the truth that has always been inside you. I hope it gives you the courage to honour your values, to speak with care, and to listen with openness — even when the world around you forgets how.

Let us walk this path together, one step at a time — toward a life led not by fear or noise, but by clarity, conviction, and a quiet sense of purpose.

AUTHOR'S NOTE

This book was born not from a single epiphany, but from a collection of ordinary, deeply human moments — moments that tested me, shaped me, and ultimately revealed who I was becoming.

Each chapter carries a piece of my own life. These are not grand revelations or dramatic turning points. They are the kind of experiences many people go through — confusion, betrayal, self-doubt, quiet victories — but rarely talk about. I have lived through them, reflected on them, and written about them in real time, while practicing the values I write about: honesty, empathy, and integrity.

I wrote this for anyone who is quietly suffering. For the person who feels overwhelmed, misunderstood, or just unsure of how to begin healing. This is your invitation to pause — to notice what is happening inside you, without judgment. Growth does not begin with perfection. It begins with awareness.

I still remember the day someone at work — a man I had known for over a year — said, without hesitation, that women should stay at home, raise children, and leave work to men. He claimed that female independence was the reason marriages were failing. I said nothing. Not because I agreed — but because I froze. A part of me thought, why argue with someone so certain in their ignorance? But another part of me felt shame. I had silenced myself in the name of keeping peace.

That moment stayed with me — not because of what he said, but because it reminded me how often we are asked to abandon ourselves quietly.

This book is my way of not staying silent anymore.

It is not a manual. It is not a lecture. It is a mirror — held up gently. I want you to see your patterns, your values, your wounds, and your strength — not through anyone else's definition of "good" or "successful," but through your own clarity.

You do not need to be perfect to be powerful.

You do not need to be loud to be right.

You just need to start by knowing yourself — truly, deeply, without influence.

And from there, everything begins.

Rimana Dollie K

INTRODUCTION

One of the hardest parts of being human is learning how to connect with people who live by values that clash with our own. Each person carries a lifetime of experiences that shape their beliefs, and while some differences are easy to accept, others feel like quiet battles we must fight alone.

You might value honesty, but your friend lies to keep the peace. You may believe in equality, yet sit across the table from a family member who thinks otherwise. These moments are more than uncomfortable — they are exhausting. They pull us into a dilemma:

- **Do I speak up and risk the relationship — or stay silent and betray myself?**

We are taught to avoid conflict, to keep the surface calm. But peace built on silence is not peace — it is self-abandonment. True strength lies not in pretending to agree, but in choosing how to respond without losing who we are.

Some relationships can be preserved through respectful boundaries. Others may need distance. Either way, recognizing differences does not mean tolerating harm. It means choosing how to protect our values while staying grounded. When we repeatedly allow others to cross us — in the name of kindness, politeness, or forgiveness — we are not being noble. We are disappearing.

This book is about not disappearing anymore.

Because real peace begins inside. And sometimes, finding that peace requires discomfort. Speaking up. Walking away. Pausing. Reassessing. Choosing again.

What Do We Mean by "Values"?

Values are not just beliefs. They are the compass inside us — pointing toward what matters most, even when the road is unclear. They guide our decisions, define our boundaries, and shape our relationships.

We do not all inherit the same values. Some are personal, shaped by our own struggles and reflections. Others are cultural, passed down through family, community, and society. Both influence who we become — but not all are meant to stay.

Two Kinds of Values

Personal Values

These arise from lived experience — hard-won truths we choose for ourselves. When you speak up for what's right, even when it's uncomfortable, you're honoring a personal value. These become our deepest integrity.

Cultural Values

These are inherited: taught through tradition, school, or society. They help us function in a group — but they are not always aligned with who we are. Respecting elders or celebrating festivals might come from cultural values. But when those values contradict our personal truths, friction arises.

How Values Shape Our Choices

Values influence everything — from the people we love to the paths we choose. Someone who values honesty will tell the truth, even if it costs them. Someone who values compassion may find purpose in helping others.

When our actions reflect our values, we feel grounded. When they do not, we feel disoriented — even if everything "looks fine" from the outside.

And sometimes, our values need to evolve. If they are rooted in fear or self-doubt, they may limit us instead of guiding us.

This book is about recognizing, reclaiming, and realigning your values — not the ones the world taught you, but the ones that speak to your truth.

From chaos to clarity.

From silence to voice.

From the edge of the breaking point to the core of who you are.

STAGE 1: FOUNDATION

(LAYING THE PHILOSOPHICAL AND EMOTIONAL GROUNDWORK)

CHAPTER 1

WHAT DOES IT MEAN TO BE GOOD? A CHILD'S QUESTION, AN ADULT'S JOURNEY

"You have to be a good boy," said the father.

The little boy paused, looked up, and asked, "What does it mean to be a good boy?"

I overheard this conversation during one of my evening walks, and it struck a chord within me.

The father responded, "A good boy goes to school every day, does his homework, and listens to his parents, always behaves properly."

It was a familiar answer – one most parents might give. But as I walked on, the question lingered in my mind.

Is that really what it means to be good? Is goodness just about doing what we are told? Following rules, meeting expectations, ticking boxes? Or is it something more profound—something rooted not in obedience, but in intention?

The Moment Led Me To Reflect

Goodness is often misunderstood. It's not just about rules or appearances. True goodness is shaped by who we are inside – our honesty, kindness, compassion, and sense of what is right. It's about being someone who makes the surroundings better, not just for ourselves but for those around us.

But the real question is, **where do we first learn these ideas?**

Most of it begins in childhood. We absorb values by watching those around us—our parents, our families, our communities. We observe how people speak to each other, how they behave when they are frustrated, and how they treat those who can't give them anything in return.

We also learn from experience. Sometimes, we learn what not to do. Sometimes, we are lucky enough to witness real integrity, and that stays with us. Our upbringing does not just shape how we act—it molds our emotional responses, our decisions, and how we relate to others. These early lessons often follow us into adulthood.

So, when we talk about being good, it's not about following a checklist. It's about asking ourselves: *What kind of person do I want to be?*

The child's question reminded me that "What does it mean to be good?" is not just a child's question. **It's a question we all need to keep asking, no matter how old we are.**

The Power Behind The Question

As children, many of us were told to "be good." But how clearly was that ever defined?

We were often praised for good grades, for being obedient, for pleasing others. But how often were we encouraged to speak the truth, to act with courage, to show quiet kindness when no one was watching?

We were punished for mistakes more often than we were guided with patience. We were taught to blend in, to keep up, to stay in line. Over time, the idea of being "good" became a performance—we are taught to follow a familiar script, earn good grades, secure a job, get married, buy a home, raise a family. And if we do all that, the world smiles and says, "You have done well." **But have we!**

Is checking every box the same as living a meaningful life? Is being a "good" person just about meeting expectations, or is it about staying true to who we are, even when that path looks different?

Somewhere along the way, many of us stop asking these questions. We confuse goodness with obedience. We equate conformity with character. And in doing so, we lose touch with what truly makes us whole.

The Inner Foundation

As children, we absorb values through the way we are treated—those early moments help shape our sense of what is right and wrong. A child raised in an environment of respect and kindness doesn't just learn these values intellectually; they feel them. And those early feelings become a moral compass, guiding their sense of right and wrong—not out of fear, but out of love, compassion, and understanding.

This is where morality begins, not as a rulebook, but as a way of being.

But as adults, we often lose sight of that foundation.

We get caught up in responsibilities, ambitions, deadlines, and everyday stress. Slowly, without realizing it, we begin to disconnect from ourselves.

What once guided our choices—our sense of fairness, kindness, and inner clarity—starts to feel distant. And when life becomes too loud, we do not always know why we feel unsettled. Often, it is because we have drifted away from that quiet inner guide—the part of us that helps align our actions with our values.

The Ordinary Moments That Matter

Real growth does not always begin with dramatic events. Sometimes it starts with the smallest decisions.

Choosing honesty when it's easier to lie.

Choosing kindness when frustration tempts you.

Choosing to listen, truly listen, instead of judging.

These small choices build a meaningful life. Over time, they shape not just moments, but who we are becoming. And life does begin to change. Not in grand sweeping gestures, but in small steady shifts. With each act of empathy, with each moment of integrity we begin to feel different. More grounded. More whole.

Teaching By Example

That little boy question reminded me that goodness is not something we define with a list. It is something we live. Values are not taught through lectures—they are felt through presence.

We learn by example. A kind word from a teacher. A small gesture from a neighbor. A quiet moment of honesty from a stranger. These moments stay with us longer than we realize.

I understood this more deeply during a visit to Manali on my 32nd birthday. I returned to a small café I had discovered during the pandemic—a tucked-away place run by a couple from Chile. The café had wooden tables painted in bright colours, the scent of fresh coffee always in the air, and a quiet charm that made you feel at ease the moment you stepped in.

The woman who ran it, **Maria**, had left a quiet impression on me the first time I visited. There was something calming about the way she interacted—gentle, attentive, with so much **love towards people and God.** You could feel the warmth in her presence.

When I walked into the café again after more than a year, her face lit up in recognition. We smiled, shared stories, and laughed. And when she learned it was my birthday, she quietly arranged a small cake just for me. No big gestures. No fuss. Just simple presence.

It was not about the cake. It was how she made me feel—seen, remembered. That kind of thoughtfulness lingers.

It tells you, that **YOU** matter.

Maria's gesture did not come from obligation. It came from who she was—shaped by values likely passed down through her own life and upbringing. And this is how values live on—not through what we say, but through what we do. Through how we treat others when no one is watching.

True goodness does not need attention. It just needs sincerity.

So what does all of this mean for us!!

It means that goodness is not something we outgrow. It's something we grow into.

That child asked a simple question—one many adults are still quietly carrying. And the answer is not found in perfection. It is in the small, consistent choices we make.

It is in how we treat others when there is nothing to gain.

It is in how we stay true to ourselves when it is hard.

To stay connected to that inner strength, here are a few gentle reminders:

Pay attention to the subtle gestures. The quiet support of a friend who simply stays. A gentle correction from a mentor who believes in you. The way someone remembers the little things about you. These moments may seem ordinary, but they shape how we experience the world.

Be forgiving—especially with yourself. We all fall short. Growth does not come from performing perfectly but from learning with compassion.

Stay curious—Let your values evolve with your experiences. Keep asking questions. Stay open to new perspectives.

Be the example—You never know who is watching, learning, or quietly looking for a reason to believe again. A small act of grace can change someone's day—or their life.

The Blueprint Of A Good Life

That little boy's question still echoes: "What does it mean to be good?"

And maybe the answer is not something we arrive all at once—but something we discover in moments.

Over the years, I have seen people change—not by doing more, but by living more truthfully. I have seen families heal, communities reconnect, and individuals become sources of quiet strength. Not through grand declarations, but by returning to their values, again and again.

So let your heart stay open. Let your inner child stay curious. And remember: **every act**

of kindness, every honest word, every thoughtful choice—these are the steps that make a life truly good.

CHAPTER 2

CHOOSING THE HARDER RIGHT OVER THE EASIER WRONG

Imagine building a house without a foundation. No matter how artistic the walls or elegant the roof, it will crumble without a strong base. Life works the same way. Integrity and honesty form the ground beneath us. They shape our choices, steady our relationships, and build real trust.

Integrity means your beliefs and behaviors match. It's not about being flawless. It's about showing up with consistency. It's like a quiet system inside us. Whether it's owning a mistake, refusing to cut corners, or being truthful with a friend—integrity and honesty keeps us steady.

I have seen people who struggle with this. You probably have too. People who seem warm on the outside but leave you unsure of where you stand.

SHRI – When Niceness Has An Agenda

Back then, she was a colleague—charming, loud, always checking in. During a rough patch in my life, she even called to ask if I needed help. It felt sincere. She talked to everyone like they were her closest friend or so it seemed.

But slowly, something felt off.

She would speak kindly to people, then quietly share their flaws when they weren't around. She would position herself as the wise one, the one who "got it," while the rest of us seemed unreliable, confused, or selfish. And yet, minutes later, she would be laughing with those same people like nothing happened. I was left confused. Was I the only one seeing this?

Then it happened to me. One day, I checked in with her—as any senior teammate would. "Let me know how it's going. I am here if you need anything." It was meant as support. Basic teamwork.

But days later, I heard she had gone to our boss: "Why is she asking me what I'm doing? She's interfering." Just a quiet complaint behind my back.

Another time, I delegated a task to one of my colleagues. My manager already knew. But Shri went straight to the colleague and asked, "Did our manager even know about this, because it seems like only Dollie is getting credit?" It sounded like concern.

These incidents made me questioned myself. Was I overreacting! But the patterns were impossible to ignore.

What seemed like concerns was not even curiosity. It was a seed of doubt. It was subtle, polished, wrapped in a soft tone with a smile. That's what made it so effective—and dangerous.

Weaponized Sweetness

It took time, but eventually, I saw it clearly. Shri was not helping me—she was managing the narrative. Positioning herself as trustworthy while quietly pulling trust away from others. She didn't need to raise her voice. Her tools were warmth, concern, and just enough doubt to make others wonder.

Not every sweet face is kind.

Not every polite voice is honest.

Some people use warmth like a disguise.

Real kindness doesn't need to control. It doesn't stir doubt or seek leverage. It supports. It empowers.

Shri's kindness had strings attached. It was not about connection—it was about control. She wasn't building relationships. She was building influence.

And that's not integrity.

Integrity means your words, actions, and motives are aligned. Shri collected trust like currency, spending it when it suited her. She thought being liked was enough. But under that surface, something was off—lacking from deeper values.

A Mirror For All Of Us

And it's not just her. Many of us fall into that trap. We confuse being liked with being kind. We stay on the surface because it feels safer. But in doing so, we drift from who we want to be.

So ask yourself:

Are your actions aligned with your values? Is your kindness rooted in sincerity—or strategy?

The Other Kind Of Quiet

How often do you meet someone who is not loud with their action, does not seek the spotlight. She works on herself not to impress, but to stay honest. One day, she was awarded a significant sum for a team project. She could have taken the credit. No one would have questioned it.

Instead, she gave the money to the team members who had done the work.

No announcement. No performance. Just quiet fairness.

No one knew—because for her, doing what's right wasn't about being seen. It was about being true.

That moment stayed with me.

It showed me what real integrity looks like: calm, quiet, and rooted—not in appearance but in purpose.

Some people wear kindness like a mask. Others carry it in their bones. They don't try to shine. They are the light.

This kind of truthfulness leads to something else: Ownership.

People with integrity do not just speak truth—they live it. They take responsibility not because someone's watching, but because they couldn't live any other way. When they make a mistake, they admit it. They reflect, adjust, and move forward.

They don't see admitting fault as weakness—it's a strength. It builds maturity. It builds trust.

When They Do Not Even Know They Are Wrong

But what happens when someone does not take ownership, when they don't even realize they have done something wrong?

That is often the case with people like Shri. They move through life wrapped in their own version of the truth, rarely pausing to question their actions. It is often out of habit, self-preservation, or simply a lack of reflection. They convince themselves they are justified, that their words did not really harm, or that their choices were necessary. This kind of behaviour does not excuse the harm caused; it simply points to a deeper issue: **a numbed sense of awareness.**

When someone stops asking themselves the hard questions, "Was I fair?" "Did I cause pain?" "Am I acting from ego or principle?" And sometimes, they never truly knew how to listen to it in the first place. What follows is not always intentional malice, but a kind of moral sleepwalking, harm born not from hatred, but from disconnection. Yet ignorance, no matter how quiet it may seem, does not lead to peace.

Just because someone remains unaware of the impact of their actions does not mean those actions are harmless or right. It simply means **they have postponed the discomfort that comes with growth**.

True peace is not born from avoidance; it is born from courage. The courage to look inward, to confront the truth, and to make things right. And that's why integrity matters so deeply. Yes, it does come with a cost.

You Will Question Your Path

Living with integrity is not always easy and will make you question your path. While you are carrying the weight of doing what's right, people like Shri seem to be flying light, twisting stories, dodging responsibility, and charming their way through life. And somehow, the world claps for them.

In such cases it is normal to ask yourself:

- *"If they're so happy being who they are, then why am I struggling just to be good?"*
- *"Why does my honesty feel like a burden, while their manipulation looks like success?"*

But pause here, and remember:

There is a world of difference between **comfort and peace.**

People like Shri might look comfortable. They laugh loudly, walk confidently, and seem to always land on their feet. Because somewhere, deep down, she knows the truth she is hiding. And no matter how loud the applause, there is always a shadow following her,

That's not peace. That is pressure.

And when the storms of life come, as they always do, those who built on truth will stand.

They may not have loud wins. But the peace they will have will be clean.

It will be truly theirs.

And one day, they will be able to look in the mirror and say:

"I didn't sell myself to succeed.»

"I didn't pretend to win."

"I chose the harder road because it led me to the person I truly want to be."

Reflect on the following when your integrity is in dilemma

1. Do you trust people too quickly based on how they make you feel?
2. When you benefit from something unearned, do you keep it or make it right?
3. Is your kindness honest or strategic?
4. Who quietly leads by example in your life?What can you learn from them?
5. Are you someone others can trust when no one is watching?

STAGE 2: DISCOMFORT

(FACING PAINFUL TRUTHS AND EMOTIONAL UPHEAVAL)

CHAPTER 3

WHY TRUTH HURTS AFTER COMFORTING LIES

A Slow Descent Into Pain

Deepshikha, a woman with a gentle spirit and a hopeful heart, believed in the power of genuine connection. When she met a colleague at work, their relationship began with small gestures and quiet conversations that made her feel safe and appreciated. For the first three months, everything seemed perfect. He was kind and attentive, and his words made her believe they were building something real together. She allowed herself to imagine a future with him, thinking that the little moments of affection were the building blocks of lasting love.

Then, one day, the truth came crashing down—he was already married. When she confronted him, he broke down in tears, explaining that he felt trapped in a marriage that was slowly unravelling and desperately wanted to start a new life with her. His emotional confession stirred a conflict within her—a struggle between her hurt and a longing to believe that love might overcome the darkness of his past.

Despite the initial shock, she chose to forgive him, holding onto the hope that love could mend the wounds of deception. They moved in together, and for a while, things seemed to improve. There were days filled with shared laughter and plans for a future where the past could be forgotten. Yet, as time went on, small red flags began to appear. Every morning at 9 and every evening at 10, his phone would ring. He would step outside to take the call, leaving her alone with her thoughts. When she asked about these calls, his tone betraying a hint of defensiveness that only deepened her unease. The comforting story he had once told her was beginning to crumble under the weight of inconsistencies and secrets.

Day after day, she battled with a rising inner conflict. Part of her wanted to leave, to free herself from the pain of constant uncertainty, but another part clung to the hope that things might change.

This daily push and pull became a routine of emotional highs and lows. Over the course of a year, the small betrayals accumulated, creating a heavy burden that was hard to shake off.

The persistent dishonesty began to wear her down. The moments of doubt slowly undermined the confidence she once had in her own judgment. Eventually, the weight of the deception led her into a deep depression. The vibrant woman who once embraced life with open arms became withdrawn and filled with a sense of despair. In search of help, she turned to therapy—a decision that marked the beginning of her long road to healing.

How Lies Transform Into Deep Emotional Wounds

The discovery of his lies did not mark the end of her pain—it was only the beginning. While she tried to rebuild the relationship, hoping honesty would follow confession, what actually followed was a more subtle, ongoing erosion of trust.

She began to notice that things still did not add up. Phone calls he would not explain, vague responses to simple questions, changes in behaviour that felt familiar in their dishonesty. At first, she dismissed these moments, telling herself that rebuilding trust would take time. But slowly, the emotional weight of constantly wondering, questioning, and doubting began to take its toll.

Each instance of dishonesty, no matter how small—had a cumulative effect. Over time, it wore down her sense of stability. What she once considered minor lapses became routine, she could no longer ignore. The man who had once made her feel safe was now the source of her deepest unease.

This ongoing uncertainty began to impact her self-worth. She stopped trusting her own judgment, replaying conversations in her mind and second-guessing her instincts. The more she tried to rationalize his behaviour, the more disconnected she felt from herself. What had started as hope turned into a quiet but persistent emotional drain, one that left her exhausted, anxious, and deeply alone within the relationship.

The Impact On Values And Self-Worth

What made the situation even more damaging was how it shook her belief system. When you enter a relationship with openness and trust, you also bring with your values, that you assume are shared. For Deepshikha, the betrayal was not limited to broken promises; it challenged the very principles she had always lived by.

These questions did not turn her bitter, but they did prompt her to reassess how she approached relationships. Trust and generosity remain important—but not at the cost of personal well-being. The experience taught her that protecting oneself is not a sign of weakness; it is a necessary act of self-respect.

Embracing The Power Of Truth

Confronting the truth, though painful, is the only path to true transformation. The lie may have offered temporary comfort, but it was the truth that ultimately set her free. When the reality of the situation became undeniable, she faced it head-on, even though it hurt deeply. That courageous act of accepting the truth marked the turning point in her journey.

By facing what she had been trying to avoid, she reclaimed control over her life. Instead of being defined by deception, she began shaping her future on the foundation of honesty and self-respect. And in doing so, she discovered something powerful—that the truth, however harsh, could cut through the fog of doubt and reveal a clearer, more grounded path forward.

But that clarity was not a finish line. It was the beginning of something harder: healing.

Clarity does not erase pain. It simply removes confusion. The emotional aftermath remains, raw and unfiltered, waiting to be faced day by day. That is the part no one prepares you for—what comes after the truth. When the denial ends, the real work begins.

A Journey Of Gradual Renewal

When you have been carrying emotional pain for a long time and have been living in the depths of that discomfort, healing takes time.

It begins not with grand resolutions but with small, steady steps. It is never a single, dramatic decision—it is a quiet commitment renewed each day: choosing to get up, choosing to keep going, and choosing to believe, however faintly, that peace is still possible.

For Deepshikha, the process was slow and often uneven. There were moments of doubt. Days marked by emotional exhaustion. And times when slipping back into old patterns felt easier than carving a new path forward.

And yet, even after recognized the truth, healing did not arrive quickly. But something inside her slowly began to shift. The strength she once lost started to resurface—not in loud declarations or dramatic changes, but in the smallest of ways.

She began setting boundaries that she avoided. She started saying "no" without guilt. She spoke up when it was needed. These were not major milestones—they were small acts of courage. But they were real.

Each moment she chose herself over fear was like planting a seed, a quiet act of healing that promised future growth. And through that steady practice, she began to reclaim not only her life—but her sense of identity, strength, and voice.

The longer you remain in a space that drains you, the deeper your wounds can grow. Starting the healing process early—however uncertain or difficult—can save you from going so deep that the way back feels impossible.

Moving Forward With Confidence

What once felt like a personal failure began to look different. She no longer viewed herself as someone who had been fooled. She saw herself as someone who chose love, who gave trust, who believed in people. And though that belief had been abused, it was not something to be ashamed of.

She realized that the experience, while painful, had sharpened her awareness. It did not make her cold—it made her discerning. It did not make her bitter—it made her learn to set boundaries. And slowly, confidence returned. A quiet knowing that she could trust herself again.

Never again she could downplay her instincts for the sake of someone else's comfort. This was not just healing—it was transformation.

What The Journey Involves

There is no neat checklist for recovering from betrayal. You are not defined by what broke your heart. You are defined by how you choose to mend it.

Let this be your turning point. Not because everything suddenly makes sense, but because you have decided you deserve more than comfort built on lies.

If you step back, certain truths begin to reveal themselves. Deepshikha's journey reflected many of them:

- **Acknowledging reality:** No more minimizing, no more rationalizing.
- **Accepting support:** Letting others see the broken pieces, without shame.
- **Reclaiming self-worth:** Defining her value not by who stayed, but by how she showed up for herself.
- **Setting and protecting boundaries:** Recognizing that peace is not selfish—it is survival.
- **Building healthier habits:** Swapping reaction with reflection.
- **Learning the lesson:** Without letting the pain take over the meaning.
- **Owning the narrative:** Telling her story from a place of strength, not victimhood.

These steps did not lead to perfection. But they led to something more important: **peace**.

Questions To Reconnect With Truth And Self-Worth

1. Have I ever chosen a comforting lie over a painful truth? What did it cost me?
2. What signs of dishonesty or emotional manipulation have I ignored in past relationships?
3. Did I question my own judgment because of someone else's repeated deceit?
4. What values did I compromise in the name of preserving peace or connection?
5. When did I first sense that something was wrong—and what stopped me from acting sooner?
6. What does "trusting myself" look like today, compared to before the betrayal?
7. How do I respond to my own emotional pain—do I suppress it, or do I allow it space to heal?
8. Am I rebuilding my life on clarity and truth, or am I still holding on to protective illusions?
9. What small actions can I take this week to strengthen my relationship with myself?
10. What would it mean to forgive myself—not for what I did, but for what I tolerated?

STAGE 3: PATTERN RECOGNITION

(UNDERSTANDING UNCONSCIOUS EMOTIONAL LOOPS AND BEHAVIOUR CYCLES)

CHAPTER 4

THE LOOP YOU DID NOT KNOW YOU WERE IN

The Comfort Of The Familiar—Even When It Hurts

There is a strange comfort in what is familiar, even when it wounds us.

Sometimes we find ourselves in the same emotional space again and again. The details may change—the people, the places, the circumstances—but the feelings echo.

A sense of rejection. A fear of not being enough. A need to prove ourselves.

We tell ourselves we have grown, but life circles back, disguised as something new, offering the same lesson until we are ready to learn.

Why does this happen?

Because the mind clings to what it knows—even when it offers us pain.

I have lived this loop.

In college, I was a quiet girl from a small town, suddenly dropped into the rush of a big city. Everything felt foreign.

The conversations, the classrooms, even the laughter. I shrank inside myself. I felt invisible.

And in that smallness, I met someone who seemed larger than life. Confident. Decisive – everything, I thought I was not.

I let him lead from where I went, what I wore, who I spoke to—all of it slowly fell under his control. At that time, it felt like care, but looking back, it was not. It was possession dressed as protection.

And with each choice he made for me, I handed over a little more of myself.

I thought love meant surrender. Because I did not yet believe I had anything worth holding onto.

Years later, I found myself in another relationship. Different man, same dynamic. He was charming, intelligent. I thought I could grow with him. But it was not long before his charm hardened into control, and control became isolation. He began to dictate everything. Eventually, it turned violent. Still, a part of me stayed—hoping he would change, or worse, believing I didn't deserve more.

What I did not realize then was this: it wasn't just about toxic people. It was about a pattern. The people changed. The emotional experience did not. I was not stuck in bad relationships—I was stuck in a loop that lived inside me.

Until I faced the fear, the self-doubt, the belief that I was not enough, I would keep attracting the same pain in different forms.

The Cycle Beneath The Surface

These loops do not just show up in love. They live in our habits with money, health, career, even the way we respond to praise or failure.

My cousin Neel is a perfect example. Smart, capable, financially stable—and always in debt.

Each time he cleared a loan, another followed. It was not because he was careless. It was something deeper.

One day I asked, "Why do you think this keeps happening?"

He paused for a long time before saying quietly, "I get anxious if I do not have more than what I grew up with."

That was his loop.

He was trying to escape the scarcity of childhood by constantly reaching for more. But in that striving, he kept recreating the very lack he feared.

This is what loops do. They make us chase what we have already survived. And unless we pause and ask, what am I really seeking? we stay trapped in motion that looks like growth—but is really a circle.

Different decisions. Same emotional root. The same lesson, knocking again.

The Courage To Pause

It is easy to keep moving—doing, fixing, striving. But patterns don't break on their own. They repeat until we interrupt them.

Neel's struggle was not about money. Just like mine was not about men, these were surface symptoms. The real drivers were hidden deeper—quiet beliefs, unconscious fears, inherited truths that had never been examined.

And to see those things clearly, you have to pause.

Awareness does not arrive through noise. It grows in silence.

Yet most of us are conditioned to avoid that stillness. We are taught to keep going, to perform, to stay ahead. But in doing so, we miss the gentle questions that offer us a way out:

- *Why do I keep choosing this?*
- *What part of me is afraid to let go?*
- *What am I trying to prove—or protect?*

We repeat patterns not because they are healthy, but because they are familiar. Even if they hurt, they feel safe. But safety and healing are not the same. Familiarity is not the same as truth.

Growth begins when you choose differently—not because it's easier, but because the cost of staying the same becomes too high.

So ask yourself:

- *Do I often find myself drawn to people who overpower or guide me?*

- *Do I make choices that leave me feeling drained—financially, emotionally, or otherwise?*
- *Even when I accomplish something, do I still feel not good enough?*

These are not accidents. They are messages. Invitations to reflect.

Because you cannot heal what you refuse to see.

And you cannot walk a new path until you understand the one you are on.

Awareness Is Where Freedom Begins

We often say, "The past is behind us." But unless we are paying attention, the past walks beside us. It lives in our decisions, hides in our reactions, and echoes in the patterns we never interrupt.

We cannot change what happened—but we can change how we carry it. That shift begins with awareness.

Awareness is rarely dramatic. It is quiet.

It is noticing how your body tenses when someone raises their voice.

How you shrink when challenged.

How do you justify harmful behaviour just because it is familiar.

These are not small moments. They are the beginning of everything.

When I finally asked myself, "*Why do I keep choosing men who control me?*"—the answer was not about them. It was about me. I did not trust my own voice. I thought I needed someone stronger to lead me, because I had not learned to lead myself.

It was uncomfortable to admit. But it was freeing.

Because once I saw it, I could not unsee it.

From there, change began. Slowly. Not perfectly. But with intention.

I started listening to my body. I began pausing before saying yes. I stayed with discomfort instead of numbing it.

Fear still visits. So does doubt. But they no longer drive me.

The same shift happened for Neel. Once he realized he was not spending from need but from memory—from the ache of never having enough—he changed. Not by punishing himself. But by asking better questions.

Do I really need this? Or am I soothing something?

That is the quiet power of awareness: it gives you back your choice. And choice is where your freedom lives.

You are Not Broken. You are Just Unaware.

So many of us carry a quiet weight:

Why does this keep happening to me?

We think we are cursed, stuck, defective.

You are just unaware.

These loops are not chains. They are patterns.

Learned behaviour. Inherited reflexes.

And anything learned can be unlearned.

The Signs Of A Loop

Before you break a pattern, you have to see it. But these loops are subtle. They do not announce themselves. They feel like ordinary life—until they don't.

Here are quiet ways to begin noticing them:

1. **Familiar Endings**
   Do you end up in similar emotional places, no matter the person or situation? If you keep feeling invisible, unappreciated, or abandoned—even with different people—it's not just coincidence. It is a pattern asking for your attention.
2. **Reflex Reactions**
   How do you respond under stress? Do you shut down, lash out, or seek approval? These reactions are not new. They are old habits disguised as instincts. If the same reaction plays out over and over, something deeper is looping.
3. **Emotional Echoes**
   Your body remembers. If certain conversations, places, or people leave you anxious, angry, or small—your nervous system is flagging a pattern. These aren't just moods. They are messages.
4. **Effort Without Change**
   You are doing the work—reading, growing, journaling. But somehow, you end up in the

same place. That is not failure. It's a sign that internal stories still hold the steering wheel. Until those shift, the destination will not.

5. **Feedback from Others**
   Sometimes the people closest to you see the loop before you do. If someone gently points out a pattern, try not to get defensive. Consider that they might be offering you a mirror.
6. **Daily Reflection**
   You do not need to solve it all today. But you do need to notice. One small pause. One quiet check-in. What did I feel today? What keeps repeating?

These small questions begin the undoing.

You are Not Stuck—You Are Standing At A Threshold

Even if you don't know the next step, choosing not to repeat the old one is a step in itself.

Every moment of awareness breaks a thread in the old loop.

Every small act of self-honesty builds the bridge to something new.

So, no—you are not stuck. You are standing at the edge of your old self, ready to meet who you are becoming.

Let that be your turning point.

Things To Think About

1. What is a recurring emotional experience in your life?
2. What belief might be feeding that pattern?
3. Can you remember a moment where you almost broke it—and what held you back?
4. Are you repeating for safety, or reaching for growth?
5. What is one response you can pause before giving this week?

You are not here to live in loops.

You are here to become whole.

STAGE 4: MORAL & ETHICAL CHALLENGES

(CONFRONTING EGO, IMAGE, AND THE NEED FOR EXTERNAL APPROVAL)

CHAPTER 5

IMAGES ARE TEMPORARY

People Rooted In Values Do Not Need To Build Temporary Images

Courage is often misunderstood. Many imagine it as loud gestures, bold speeches, or headline-worthy choices. But real courage is not always visible. It does not need to be seen or praised. It shows up quietly—in everyday choices, steady principles, and the way a person carries themselves when no one is watching.

People who are clear about their values do not waste energy trying to perform for others. They do not craft temporary versions of themselves just to fit in. They do not adjust their voice to match the room or tailor their opinions to gain approval. They are who they are—consistently. This is not about how you carry yourself physically. **It is not about improving your communication**

or grooming your personality. What I am talking about is different—**it is the quiet, habitual act of hiding.** Of creating a version of yourself shaped by the need to be liked, accepted, or praised.

When we are not grounded inside, we often chase that outside. We curate our image carefully, hoping to be liked, respected, or noticed. We try to appear more successful, more confident, more "together" than we actually feel. It might work in the short term. But eventually, those images fade. Because what is built for appearance has no permanence. It disappears the moment circumstances change.

True courage is not found in how we present ourselves. It is shaped by how we see ourselves—and how deeply we trust our reasons for showing up the way we do.

Live With Quiet Strength

One of the clearest examples of quiet courage I have seen through Sita, our house help. She does not have formal education or social advantages. But she moves through life with calm assurance and a steady sense of dignity.

She never asks for praise. She does not try to impress anyone. Her presence is simple, consistent, and self-assured. I remember once grumbling to her about the cook making a mess in the kitchen. **Without pausing, she smiled and said, "Madam, be grateful there's food on the table. A mess can be cleaned with a smile."**

That moment lingered with me—not as a simple reminder to be grateful, but as a lesson in perspective, grace, and maturity. Her words carried clarity, not from books or training—but from lived experience. She did not say it to correct me. It was not for effect. That is just how she thinks. That is how deeply her values guide her.

Even during personal or financial difficulty, she never asked for sympathy. She did not dramatize. She did not shrink. She did not need others to validate her strength—because it was not built on performance. It came from who she was, not how she looked to others.

When Fear Wears A Mask

In contrast, I remember Vinita from my dance class. Outwardly, she had it all—good looks, confidence, success. But underneath, there was a constant need for reassurance.

She would call late at night, asking, "Was anyone talking about me today?" or "How do I come across to people?" She did not sound arrogant—she sounded anxious. In class, she laughed loudly and said things like, "I don't care what people think." But it was clear that she did care. A lot.

Sometimes, even without context, she would look at me and ask quietly,

"How do I come across to people?"

Vinita was not pretending to be someone else—she was trying to survive. A little safer, a little more accepted. Performance was her shield. Every shift in tone, every exaggerated smile, was a quiet plea for safety in a world that had taught her she was not enough as she was.

She became what each room needed her to be, not out of deceit, but out of fear that her real self might not be enough.

But that kind of constant performance is exhausting. And it never brings peace.

Vinita was not missing ability—she was missing grounding. Her sense of worth depended entirely on others' opinions. As long as she kept looking outside for validation, she could not find stability within herself.

This is more common than we admit. So many people today are not focused on becoming better—they are focused on appearing better. They say the right things, post polished thoughts, and try to look like they are doing well. But that's not growth. That is image management. And over time, it starts to feel empty.

Real confidence does not shift based on who is watching. It is steady because it comes from within. And that kind of courage does not need to be announced.

Root Yourself In Truth

Growing up is not just about age. It is about becoming aware of how much of your behaviour is driven by fear—fear of rejection, of not being enough, of being unseen.

We all try on versions of ourselves. We want to be liked. We want to feel safe. That is human. But at some point, you must ask: *Am I performing, or am I being real?*

Your values become your anchor. When you are not sure who you are, every opinion can shake you. Every stare can make you shrink. But when you are grounded in clarity—kindness, honesty, dignity—you stop bending to match the moment. You stop acting. You start being.

Both Sita and Vinita taught me that. One through her stillness, the other through her struggle. One showed me what it looks like to live with quiet confidence. The other revealed how tiring it is to keep reshaping yourself just to feel seen.

Courage Is Not Loud

Courage is not about being noticed. It is about staying true to yourself—even when that truth earns you nothing. It is choosing to respond with respect when it is easier to react with anger. It is being kind without needing credit. And it is letting go of image, because truth matters more.

Sita never called herself **strong.** But her actions made it clear.

Vinita never said she was afraid. But her questions revealed what she was **battling inside**.

As for me—I have come to understand that courage is not something we either have or do not.

It is a habit. A daily decision. A quiet practice of showing up without disguise.

Reflection: Ask Yourself Honestly

1. Who in your life reminds you of Sita—someone who leads through quiet values?
2. Have you ever caught yourself trying to shape an image instead of standing in your truth?
3. What values matter to you most—and do your actions reflect them?
4. What part of yourself are you hiding to fit in?
5. Where are you still performing?
6. What would change if you let that image go?

CHAPTER 6

UNDERSTAND YOUR SELF-WORTH

Valuing Yourself: The Foundation Of A Meaningful Life

How much do you truly value yourself?

Do you remind yourself that you are capable, deserving, and enough? Or do you constantly question whether you are good enough?

For years, I did not fully understand what it meant to value myself. Like many people, I based my self-worth on external validation—on how others perceived me, my career success, and how well I met societal expectations. But over time, I began to see the truth: when we do not value ourselves internally, we hand over that power to the world around us. And that can lead to a cycle of imbalance, dissatisfaction, and emotional emptiness.

Where Worth Gets Distorted

The corporate world teaches many things, but perhaps its most consistent lesson is about how easily self-worth gets tangled in professional performance. We are conditioned to believe that our job title, salary, or promotion defines who we are. Somewhere along the way, we forget that we are more than just our job titles.

I have watched people work themselves to the edge—sacrificing their health, relationships, and mental peace—just to meet shifting expectations. They stay late, burn out, and still wonder if it is enough. When targets are missed or recognition does not come, their confidence collapses.

Why? **Because their value is attached to outcomes instead of identity.** We are taught to be productive, to prove our worth through results, but rarely do we learn to ask ourselves: *Who am I outside of my job? What do I love? What truly brings me happiness?*

During my 9-to-5 job, I worked under a manager who perfectly reflected this dysfunction. His priority was always the client, never the team. He enjoys dominating others, speaking in a way that makes it clear he finds superiority in demeaning people. Conversations with him are one-sided, he talks, but others do not get a chance to speak. If he asks a question, everyone is expected to have an answer. But if we ask him something, he only responds when it suits him.

The environment drained us. I saw fatigue in my colleagues' faces. I felt it too. But instead of questioning the system, we questioned ourselves.

This is where self-value becomes crucial. You start to believe that tolerating toxicity is necessary for survival. But is success a really success if it empties your spirit?

In workplaces, you will find many who seek validation through power and control. People who dictate to others, micromanage, or seek dominance often do so to satisfy their ego. They believe that controlling others will make them feel more important. However, this sense of power is short-lived. It does not bring long-term fulfilment but instead deepens the void within. True empowerment does not come from controlling others; it comes from valuing yourself and elevating others around you.

Your Life Is What You Make It

For the longest time, I believed success meant earning approval—fitting into molds, exceeding expectations, and proving my worth. But real success is not a performance. It is living with intention—beyond checklists, titles, and applause.

The pressure of corporate life began to dull something inside me. Each day felt like a transaction—perform, deliver, repeat. But beneath the routines and expectations, there was another part of me waiting—a quieter truth I had long ignored.

That shift began when I leaned into my passion for modelling. Despite the demands of my corporate job, I refused to let that part of me go quiet. I prepared, practiced, and stepped out of routine—and **in 2023, I won the Mrs. India Asia title.**

It was not just a crown. A moment of self-ownership. A line drawn between the version of me who needed permission—and the one who finally realized she never had to ask for it.

That day reminded me that we are not bound by the roles we play in one part of our lives. We can define success on our terms. We can be many things—graceful and grounded, ambitious and soft, bold and kind—all at once. You always have choices. You can speak up, set limits, or pursue something beyond your job. The only reason we stay stuck is that we forget our worth.

More Than Success: The Role of Morals And Behaviour

In the race to succeed, many people focus only on proving themselves right, defending their opinions, or winning arguments—often at the cost of relationships and basic human kindness. Success is not just about being the smartest in the room, it is also about how you treat people along the way.

Your words and actions stick with people forever. You may forget what you said in a moment of anger or frustration, but the person on the receiving end might carry that hurt for years. **Do not be the reason someone skips a meal because of stress, hates waking up in the morning because of anxiety, or feels left out and unworthy and most importantly loses confidence on themselves.**

What is the point of success if, in the process, you step on others to get there? If your achievements come at the cost of kindness and compassion, is it really success? True growth comes when we improve not just in skills and knowledge but also in our morals, values, and behaviour towards others.

Instead of proving yourself right all the time, try to understand others. Instead of feeding your ego by controlling people or situations, focus on lifting others up. A truly successful person is someone who not only excels in their career but also leaves a positive impact on the people around them.

So how do we shift from surviving to self-valuing?

Let us break it down.

Step 1: Self-Awareness – Rewriting the Internal Dialogue

Everything begins with self-talk. If you constantly feel "not good enough," ask yourself:

- *Where did this belief come from?*
- *Whose voice is it really?*

Toxic environments feed us unspoken rules:

- I must tolerate mistreatment to be successful.
- If I speak up, I will lose everything.
- My worth depends on my performance.

But these thoughts do not come from truth. They come from conditioning.

Self-awareness means noticing these thoughts—and questioning them. Then, you rewrite them:

- I am valuable because of who I am—not just what I do.
- I deserve to be in spaces where I am respected.
- I have the right to create a life beyond this job.

When your internal narrative changes, your external decisions follow.

Step 2: Creating Balance – A Life Beyond Work

Many people believe their career is their only identity. Their self-worth rises and falls with their job performance.

But I have learned that meaning comes from balance—not burnout.

That Mrs. India Asia title was not just a personal win. It was proof that life has room for more than routine. That we are allowed to follow passions, chase joy, and still show up professionally.

Ask yourself:

- *What brings me joy outside of work?*
- *When was the last time I did something just for myself?*
- *Am I living, or just getting through the week?*

You do not need to abandon your job. You need to expand your identity beyond it. Hobbies, relationships, and wellness all deserve space. They are not extras—they are essentials.

Step 3: Setting Boundaries – Taking Back Your Power

Toxic workplaces flourish where boundaries are missing.

When you say yes to everything, people assume it is okay to take more. And soon, your time, energy, and emotional bandwidth are gone.

Valuing yourself means learning when to say No–It means protecting your focus, not just your deliverables.

Here is how you start:

- Decline work that consistently violates your well-being.
- Resist the urge to over-deliver just to be liked.
- Block time for rest, creativity, or just breathing space.

You Control Your Life

Your manager does not define your story. Your job title does not set your value.

What does? The choices you make.

When you begin choosing yourself—your joy, your peace, your balance—everything shifts. You stop asking for permission to feel whole. You start acting like you deserve more.

Because you do.

You make and break your own life. So, build something that reflects not just what you can do—but who you are. When the external world spins—deadlines shift, titles change, people come and go—it is your inner compass that brings you home. Without it, you drift, pulled by currents you did not choose. With it, you move with clarity, even when the road is unclear.

Ask yourself:

- *What direction am I really headed in?*
- *Am I living by others' coordinates—or my own?*

If the answers feel off, take a moment to recalibrate.

Work is a chapter—not the whole book. Make space for family, health, creativity, rest, and joy. Let your life feel full, not just look impressive.

The Freedom Of Self-Value

When you truly value yourself, you free yourself.

You stop chasing validation. You stop performing. You start choosing—with clarity and conviction.

Valuing yourself is not just about self-love—it is about recognizing that your life is bigger than any single role you play. It is about embracing all parts of yourself and creating a life that feels fulfilling, not just impressive on paper.

Reflection: Ask Yourself Honestly

1. Where have I attached my value to performance or approval?

2. What beliefs have shaped how I see myself? Are they still true?
3. How do I treat myself when I fall short?
4. What would it look like to value myself without any external validation?

STAGE 5: EXPANDING OUTWARD

(DEVELOPING DEEPER, MORE INTENTIONAL RELATIONSHIPS AND HANDLING EXTERNAL REACTIONS)

CHAPTER 7

CULTIVATING MEANINGFUL CONNECTIONS AND RELATIONSHIPS

Life is filled with a series of encounters—some brief, others long-lasting. Every person who crosses our path has a role to play, shaping our thoughts, our values, and even our direction. Whether someone brings support or difficulty, their presence contributes to our growth. Instead of resisting these arrivals and departures, we can choose to feel grateful—for the timing, the lessons, and the movement.

The People Who Come And Go

We often hold tightly to the people we feel connected, imagining that those bonds will stay intact forever. But life shifts. Sometimes people leave—not because they stopped caring, but because their purpose in our life has been fulfilled. As difficult as it may be, losing someone we were close to often signals that a chapter has ended. It doesn't take away from the meaning they held, but it reminds us that change is part of the process.

Think about a mentor who helped you through a challenging season, or a therapist who offered clarity and support. When the time was right, they stepped away because their role was complete. Similarly, friendships and relationships that fade often leave behind valuable insights. **These transitions create space for new relationships and renewed growth.**

Lessons From Every Encounter

Every person teaches us something. Some teach through care, warmth, and consistency. Others through conflict, disappointment, or distance. Both are valuable. A kind person can help set a new standard for how we want to be treated. Someone who hurts us might teach us how to spot patterns, set firmer boundaries, or value ourselves more.

When you look back at past relationships, the goal isn't always to understand "why" something happened. The better question is, "What did this experience teach me?" Did it help you become more patient, assertive, or self-aware? If you are willing to look closely, every experience leaves something behind—something that prepares you for what comes next.

Renee's Journey: The Power Of Support

In 2015, when I was leading a team at a multinational company, a new team member named Renee joined us. I noticed her right away—quiet, polite, always composed, but her eyes carried a sadness that felt hard to miss. She never joined casual conversations or shared personal stories. Still, her presence was consistent and respectful.

Curious and concerned, I began inviting her to lunch. In the beginning, she only spoke about work. One day, we shared a ride home. She had been quiet during the drive, but something in her expression shifted. Her eyes welled up, and I gently asked, "Renee, are you okay? What is going on?"

In that moment, she opened up. She told me that shortly after her wedding, her husband confessed that he had been in another relationship all along and had no intention of building a life with her. He did not offer love or trust. And then, things took an even darker turn—he gave her poison. She slipped into a coma for three months. When she woke up, much of her memory was gone. Her entire life had changed, and she was left trying to make sense of the betrayal and pain.

I was stunned by her story. And deeply moved. I knew from that moment that I would show up for her in every way I could. Not just as a manager, but as a person. I made time to talk with her, whenever she needed someone to listen.

Over the next three years, Renee's journey slowly shifted. She began opening up more often, smiling a little brighter, engaging more with the team. The changes weren't dramatic—but they were steady. Healing took time, and there were still days when old pain resurfaced. But I saw her rebuild herself. One moment at a time.

Eventually, Renee found love again—with someone who respected and valued her. Her story became a reminder to me of what presence, patience, and empathy can do. It showed me that being there for someone doesn't require big gestures. It only requires consistency and care.

Why Her Story Matters

Renee's experience isn't just about personal trauma. It shows how deeply our lives are shaped by the people around us. It reminds us that even when someone seems okay on the outside, they may be carrying far more than we realize.

Supporting someone through pain is not about solving their problems. It's about giving them the space to be heard, respected, and seen. When you create space for someone else, you also grow. You learn patience. You practice compassion. And you learn to be present, without controlling the outcome.

It also showed me something else: the contrast between nurturing relationships and harmful ones. Toxic relationships—whether romantic or platonic—can break a person from the inside. But even then, **with the right support, people can recover and rebuild.**

Recognizing And Exiting Toxic Relationships

I experienced this firsthand. A few years ago, I thought I had found a close friend—someone I could trust with my dreams and struggles. We grew close quickly and eventually decided to live together. It felt natural. Our bond seemed unshakable.

But the change was not sudden. At first, her closeness felt nurturing. Then, it started to demand exclusivity. If I spent time with other friends or pursued my own interests, she grew distant. I would return home to cold silence—deliberate, punishing. Sometimes she would hint that I was neglecting her, making me question if I had done something wrong.

When I tried to explain my need for space or independence, the conversation twisted. She played the victim, and I was left feeling selfish. I began to doubt my choices. I walked on eggshells. I stopped reaching out to others. The apartment, once filled with warmth, now felt like a trap.

That emotional toll was real. I began to lose touch with myself. I was not just overwhelmed—I was exhausted. And it was in those quiet moments of reflection that the truth became clear: I was not the problem. I was in a friendship that no longer respected who I was.

Acknowledging that was not easy, but it was necessary. Moving away was not an act of betrayal—it was an act of reclaiming my well-being that I had learnt the hard way from my previous experiences.

Identifying Subtle Red Flags

The first step toward healing from a toxic relationship is recognizing the signs. But this is rarely obvious when you are in the middle of it. Toxicity doesn't always announce itself through conflict or cruelty—it shows up quietly, through repeated patterns that wear you down over time.

In my case, the signs weren't loud, but they were consistent.

At first, it was her need for constant closeness. It felt flattering, even comforting, to have that kind of bond. But soon, it became possessiveness. Not in words, but in energy. I would return home to silence, subtle jabs, or a vague sense.

Then came the guilt-tripping. If I expressed a need for space or balance, the conversation was turned around. She made it seem as though I was abandoning her, that I was the one being selfish. The more I tried to hold on to other friendships, the more she tightened her grip—disguised as emotional dependency. It was not concern; it was control.

There were no screaming or dramatic scenes. Just a steady erosion of my emotional freedom. A deepening doubt in myself. A constant, unspoken pressure to shrink who I was to make space for her needs.

And the hardest part? It was confusing. Because mixed with all of this were moments of genuine laughter, warmth, and shared memories. That's what made it so difficult to name the relationship as toxic. But the emotional toll was undeniable.

Here are the patterns I came to recognize—not just in her, but in any relationship that damages rather than supports:

Possessiveness masked as closeness

When someone demands exclusivity and sees your other relationships as threats, it is not loyalty—it's control. This possessiveness is a common sign of toxicity in any relationships, as it indicates an inability to respect personal boundaries.

When your need for independence is punished through cold silence or passive aggression, it's a tool of manipulation.

Victimhood to avoid accountability

If every honest conversation ends with you feeling like the villain and them the victim, that's not communication—it's distortion. This constant shifting of blame is a hallmark of toxic behaviour, where one-person never takes responsibility for their actions and instead, always casts themselves as the suffering victim.

Emotional exhaustion after each interaction

A healthy relationship might challenge you, but it never leaves you consistently depleted.

Manipulation wrapped in affection

Toxic people rarely come across as villains. Their manipulation is quiet, persuasive, and hard to detect until you've internalized it.

If you walk away from conversations feeling confused, guilty, or diminished—pause. These aren't just passing moods. They are signals. Pay attention. Because clarity begins with recognition.

The Cost Of Staying Too Long

Toxic relationships, especially those that start strong, can cloud your judgment. You begin justifying their behavior. You tell yourself it will get better. You avoid conflict to "keep the peace." But the longer you stay, the more you lose yourself.

The emotional damage can be deep. You start to second-guess your thoughts. You withdraw from others. You sacrifice your needs. And often, you stop dreaming — because survival becomes the focus.

This is why recognizing toxicity early matters. It is not just about avoiding discomfort. It is about preserving your self-worth.

Building Stronger Boundaries Going Forward

Boundaries aren't about keeping people out. They are about protecting what matters — your time, energy, and peace of mind.

To set healthy boundaries:

Know Your Limits: Pay attention to what drains or depletes you. Your discomfort is often a signal.

Be Clear and Direct: Don't leave room for assumptions. Say what you need in simple terms.

Be Consistent: Boundaries lose power when they're inconsistently enforced. Stick to what you say, even when it feels uncomfortable.

Practice Saying No: Especially if you tend to please others. Start small — a declined invitation, a delayed reply — and build from there.

Seek Help When Needed: If the person resists or manipulates your boundaries, talk to someone you trust. Reinforcement helps when your resolve is low.

Setting boundaries is not a one-time event. It's a lifelong skill — a reflection of your self-respect.

Developing A Relationship With Yourself

When you learn to develop a relationship with yourself that is where it's easier to set boundaries with toxic people. The relationship with yourself matters because it sets the tone for how others treat you and how you move through the world.

Start by becoming more self-aware. Observe your thoughts and feelings. Ask yourself what you need, not just what others expect of you.

Practice self-compassion. Speak to yourself the way you would a close friend — with understanding, not harshness. Forgive yourself. Celebrate small wins. Be patient with your process.

Prioritize self-care. It is not just about rest. It's about making time for the things that make you feel whole — whether that is a walk, a hobby, or saying no to something that drains you.

The more you nurture your inner life, the less dependent you become on external validation. You stop bending to please others. You begin to live in alignment with who you are — not who others need you to be. From that space, you no longer seek permission—you set the terms.

That inner clarity is what prepares you to face hard truths. And sometimes, the hardest truth is knowing when to let go.

Embracing Change And Moving Forward

Letting go of a relationship—especially one that was once meaningful—is rarely easy. Even when you know it is hurting you, walking away can feel like a loss. A breakup of identity, routine, and shared history.

But over time, I have come to understand that change doesn't mean failure. It means growth. Some relationships end not because we are doing something wrong, but because we are finally doing something right—choosing peace, truth, or self-respect over comfort.

And yet, moving on does not always feel like liberation at first. Sometimes, it feels like grief. You grieve not just the person, but the version of yourself that stayed too long, the hope you held on to, the effort you invested. That grief is valid. It's part of the process.

Reflection: Questions To Revisit Your Relationships

1. How do I feel before and after spending time with this person? Energized or depleted?

2. Are my relationships reciprocal, or do I feel like I am constantly giving?
3. What parts of myself do I shrink or hide to keep the peace with them?
4. Have I been ignoring red flags or dismissing discomfort as "normal"?
5. What boundaries would protect my emotional health—and am I honouring them?
6. These are not just questions—they are invitations. To pause. To notice. To come home to yourself.

CHAPTER 8

NOT EVERYONE WILL CELEBRATE YOUR SUCCESS

We often believe that the people who support us during tough times will naturally be the same ones who stand by us when things go well. It is comforting to think that emotional support during struggle also means shared celebration during success. But that's not always how things turn out.

When you are going through heartbreak, illness, or personal hardship, people often know how to show up. They offer comforting words, encouragement, or simply listen. There is a clear script in those moments—empathy feels natural.

But the reaction can shift when something good happens—when you are recognized publicly, when your work is seen, when a personal goal is reached. In those moments, you expect celebration, messages of joy, or even a few simple words of acknowledgment. Instead, what you sometimes receive is silence.

I experienced this personally on the day I was crowned Mrs. India Asia 2023. It was a moment of pride. The cameras were flashing, the applause was loud, and congratulatory messages were flooding in. I felt like I had achieved something significant.

But amid all that recognition, I noticed something unexpected. Some of the people I had once leaned on—the ones who encouraged me when I doubted myself, who had shown genuine concern during my hard times—were completely silent. No message. No call. Nothing.

As days passed and their silence remained, it became clear that this was not just forgetfulness. It was avoidance.

That moment forced me to reflect more deeply. I was not upset because I needed praise. I was unsettled by the contrast—the same people who had once comforted me when I was down had nothing to say when I stood tall.

And it raised a question that became the core of this chapter:

Why does success sometimes create distance, even from the people who once cared the most?

The Moment Of Realization – Silence In Celebration

I was not looking for public praise—I had already received that. I was looking for something quieter and more personal: a simple message, a short call, even a few words from people I considered close.

I started to question what the connection was really built on. Did they only know how to support struggle, but not success? Did they only feel comfortable when I was vulnerable, but unsure of how to relate to me when I was confident?

This was not about wanting constant applause. It was about understanding the shift. When someone goes quiet during your most visible moment, it challenges your assumptions. It makes you revisit past conversations, shared experiences, and moments of trust. You wonder if the support you received during hard times was rooted in empathy—or something else.

That moment became a turning point for me. I stopped asking, "*Why didn't they say anything?*" *and started asking something more important:*

What does this silence reveal about our relationship?

It was no longer just about a missed message. It was about realizing that not everyone is comfortable with your progress. And sometimes, the people who once stood beside you may quietly step back—not out of dislike, but out of their own unresolved emotions.

That silence lingered in my heart. And it made me wonder. why do some people vanish when joy arrives?

Understanding The Reasons Behind The Silence

When people do not respond to your success, it is easy to assume jealousy or resentment. But silence is not always driven by hostility. More often, it reflects unresolved emotions within the other person—feelings they may not fully understand themselves.

By trying to understand these deeper reasons, **you gain perspective.** You stop personalizing the silence and start seeing it as a signal of something else. Here are a few common reasons why people struggle to respond when you succeed:

1. Hidden Comparison

Your success might tap on someone's self-doubt—softly, but sharply. Not because you took anything from them, but because suddenly, they feel behind.

They might not even realize it at first. But something inside begins to whisper:

"Why not me?"

"What am I doing wrong?"

The silence that follows is not always about envy. Often, it is about shame—quiet, unspoken, and hard to admit.

2. Scarcity Mindset

Some people believe that success is limited. They think if someone else wins, there is less left for them. This is not logical—but it is a mindset many people develop from an early age. Instead of seeing your success as inspiring or shared, they see it as something that reduces their own chances.

This can make even kind people react with hesitation or discomfort when they see someone close to them doing well. They may not realize it, but their silence is shaped by fear—fear of not being seen, or of being left behind.

3. Insecurity in the Spotlight

Your progress can unintentionally highlight someone else's insecurities. When you grow or achieve something meaningful, it brings attention to areas in their life where they feel stuck. They are not upset with you—they are struggling with themselves.

We tend to mistake silence for disapproval or envy. But often, what we are witnessing is someone wrestling with their own emotions—feelings they have not fully processed, and might not even understand themselves. It is not that they do not want to be happy for you—it is that they do not know how to access their own sense of joy in that moment.

I saw this dynamic unfold in my own life; in a way I did not expect.

I became a news anchor for a local channel in Assam while I was quite young. For someone my age, it was a major milestone, and it made my parents incredibly proud. No one in my immediate circle had done anything like that before. But I noticed a shift within people.

One of my closest friends grew distant. She would not initiate conversations anymore, and when we did speak, her voice carried a strange flatness. I finally asked her what was wrong.

She paused, then said something I have never forgotten:

"I do not feel bad for you. But when I see you on TV, I feel like I should be doing something big too. I want my parents to be proud like yours are. But I do not know what to do."

We were just kids. She was not jealous, she was lost. My success had become a mirror, reflecting her inner confusion. And she did not know how to face it, much less celebrate mine.

Over the years I learned from that moment: **Not every silence is rooted in envy.**

Sometimes, it is quiet pain. The kind that stays hidden until someone has the courage—or the space—to name it.

4. Shifting Relationship Roles

Sometimes, people get used to a certain dynamic in the relationship. If they have always been the helper, the listener, or the one offering support, it can be hard for them to adjust when you are the one in a new position of strength.

They might not know how to relate to this version of you. It does not mean they do not care—it means they are unsure how to be part of this new chapter in your life. When you succeed, it changes the rhythm, and not everyone adjusts smoothly.

5. Lack of Emotional Skills

Sometimes, silence in response to your success is not about envy or discomfort—it is about not knowing what to say. Not everyone grows up learning how to express encouragement, celebrate someone else's wins, or even recognize their own joy.

Some people simply have not been taught how to say things like, "I'm really happy for you," or "That's such a great achievement." It is not that they do not care—**it is that they are unfamiliar with the language of celebration.**

Often, they have never had their own successes acknowledged. They may have learned to downplay their happiness, or felt that celebrating themselves was inappropriate or boastful. So, when someone else has a moment of joy, they freeze—not because they do not feel proud, but because they have never practiced showing it.

This lack of emotional experience can create awkward silences, missed opportunities to connect, and moments that feel colder than they actually are. **But understanding this does not excuse it—it helps you stop taking it personally.**

When Their Silence Speaks—What Should You Do?

Once you notice someone's silence during a moment that mattered to you—especially a moment of success—it is natural to feel disappointed. That lack of acknowledgment can feel personal.

What now? Should I still hold space for them in my life?

But before you make any decisions, take time to assess the relationship and how you want to move forward.

There is no universal answer for how to respond. It depends on the context, the pattern of the relationship, and your own emotional boundaries. This section offers a way to think through your response.

Start With an Honest Conversation

If the relationship matters to you, do not assume the worst. People make mistakes. Instead of cutting them off, consider having a calm and direct conversation. You might say:

"I noticed you did not say anything when I shared my news. It meant a lot to me, and I just want to check in—are we okay?"

This is not about confronting them harshly. It is about creating space for honesty. You are not demanding praise—you are looking for clarity. Their response will tell you what you need to know. If they acknowledge it, explain themselves, or apologize, there may still be room for growth in the relationship.

Look for Patterns, Not One-Time Gaps

Everyone slips up sometimes. A missed message or a slow reply does not always mean something deeper.

But if someone consistently disappears when good things happen to you, or changes the subject when you talk about your progress—that is a sign.

Supportive relationships include both comfort during struggles and celebration during wins. If someone is only present when you are low—but absent when you rise—take note. It is not about one moment. It is about repeated behaviour.

Protect Your Joy with Clear Boundaries

If their silence continues or you feel emotionally drained after interactions, consider setting boundaries. You do not have to share your accomplishments with everyone—especially not with people who do not receive them well.

This does not mean shutting people out. It means being selective about who has access to your personal moments. Treat your joy with care. It is okay to protect it.

You might start sharing your wins with people who consistently uplift you and reduce what you share with those who respond with distance or discomfort.

Know When to Let Go

Sometimes, even after conversations and patience, a relationship no longer supports who you are becoming. Letting go of someone does not always mean they did something terrible—it might just mean you have outgrown the connection.

Letting go can bring sadness. But it can also bring peace. It allows you to make room for people who meet you with genuine care—during the hard days and the good ones.

If someone cannot stand beside you when you are growing, you do not have to carry that disappointment forward. You deserve people who recognize and value your growth.

And when you stop trying to convince someone to care, space opens—for peace, for clarity, for someone new.

Letting Go, Letting In

Letting go is not always about conflict. Sometimes, it is quiet acceptance—the realization that not everyone is meant to stay through every version of your growth. As your life expands, some people step back, not out of anger, but out of unfamiliarity. And if you keep holding on, your peace begins to pay the price.

Letting go does not erase history. It just means choosing not to carry what no longer aligns with your present. It is making room—for people who meet you where you are, not where you used to be.

At the same time, remain open to letting new people in. Focus on building relationships with those who support you during your lows and show up when you are doing well. These people add value to your life and contribute to your sense of stability.

Your social circle does not have to be large, but it should be made up of people who genuinely care. People who clap for you not out of obligation, but because they mean it. Keep those people close. They are the ones who help you stay grounded and motivated.

Be The Friend, You Wish You Had

Your experience does not have to make you guarded. It can make you generous.

Silence or distance from others does not have to harden you—it can teach you something valuable. Let it be a moment of reflection: *How do I show up for the people in my life when they succeed? Do I let them know I see them?*

If someone around you is doing well, do not hold back. Celebrate their progress—whether big or small. A message, a call, a few kind words. **Most people do not want praise—they just want to feel seen.**

How you support others does not just reflect your character—it shapes your environment. The way you show up sets a tone. In healthy relationships, people grow together. Support is not a transaction. It is a choice to believe there is enough room for everyone to shine.

Things To Think About

To reflect more deeply on how success and silence show up in your own life and relationships, consider the following questions:

1. Who supported you during your most difficult time? How did they show it?
2. Who genuinely celebrated your wins? How did that feel?
3. Have you ever held back from celebrating someone else's success? Why?
4. Is there a relationship where you have felt distant after your success?
5. How do you usually express happiness for others?
6. Is there someone you need to thank or acknowledge this week?

These questions are meant to help you think clearly about your support system—and how you can continue building meaningful connections with others and with yourself.

CHAPTER 9

WHEN BEING APPROACHABLE BECAME LIFE-SAVING

Am I Truly Approachable!

Have you ever paused and asked yourself, Am I truly approachable? Not just polite or friendly on the surface, but someone others feel emotionally safe with. Someone people can come to, share honestly without the fear of being judged, dismissed, or misunderstood?

It is a question we do not often ask, but it is one of the most important things. Because being unapproachable is not always about having a bad attitude. Sometimes, it is about a quiet wall we build around ourselves—without realizing it. And that wall can cost us a lot: honest feedback, deeper connections, mutual respect, and even opportunities to grow.

Being unapproachable does not always come with anger or arrogance. Sometimes it wears a smile. Sometimes it sounds soft-spoken. But the result is the same—people hold back, stay silent, or start to withdraw.

This became clearer during one of my most fearful moments.

Hidden Essence Of Approachability

Not long ago, I was admitted to the hospital for a cervical biopsy. I had been struggling with a serious infection, and my doctor told me the procedure had to be done right away. That news alone was frightening, but what made it harder was my deep fear towards hospitals and the whole environment. This fear I have carried since childhood—one I have never fully processed.

This fear was one of the reasons I choose to run marathons. I thought that if I stayed fit and strong, maybe I would never have to deal with hospitals. But this time, there was no way around it.

I had met a doctor a few times before the procedure. Each visit left a calmness that I did not expect. There was something in the way she spoke that felt steady and kind. She did not rush. She did not overwhelm. She had a presence that gave me space to breathe.

The day of the surgery, I completely broke down. My chest was tight. My heart was racing. I was crying in the waiting room, thinking, I do not know how I am going to get through this.

Then I saw her in the operation theatre.

She did not say much. But her presence changed everything. The fear did not disappear, but it stopped spiralling. Something about her made me feel safer. Not because she had all the answers. But because she did not pull away from my panic. She did not brush it off. She did not try to fix it with words. She simply made space for it.

That was the moment **I understood what true approachability looks like.**

It is not about being cheerful or always knowing what to say. It is about being someone who creates emotional safety. Someone who can sit with you—even in silence—and make you feel like you do not have to hide what you are going through.

That day, the doctor did not just help me through a medical procedure. She reminded me what it means to feel seen, respected, and held without judgment.

Her approach that day stayed with me—and it made me notice where that presence was missing in everyday relationships.

Why This Matters More Than We Realize

In everyday life, we interact with many people—friends, partners, family, colleagues, leaders. With some, conversations feel natural. You can speak openly without hesitation. With others, even simple communication feels difficult, as though you are walking on a tightrope. You are careful with your words, unsure of how they will react.

That is why approachability matters. It is not just a personality trait. It is a choice we make in how we show up with others. It is a skill that shapes the quality of our relationships—at home, at work, and everywhere in between.

Being approachable means more than being friendly. It means being emotionally available. It means listening without rushing to correct. It means creating space for someone to express how they feel—even if what they are saying is uncomfortable or inconvenient.

In many relationships—whether romantic, platonic, or professional—the problem is not a lack of love or respect. **It is the absence of emotional safety**. One person does not feel free to speak up, to share how they really feel, or to raise concerns without being met with tension or silence.

I have seen relationships where one partner keeps everything to themselves, not because they want to hide, but because the other partner does not feel like someone they can open to. There is no room for vulnerability, only caution. And that distance slowly replaces connection.

I have seen workplaces suffer under leadership that looks **efficient on paper** but **lacks openness in practice**. I once had a colleague named Ano. I supported her work and tried to offer helpful feedback when needed. But one day, I pointed out a small issue in a project—and her entire attitude shifted. She began avoiding conversations and treating me like a threat. It became clear that she was not able to separate feedback from personal attack. It had nothing to do with the suggestion and everything to do with how she saw herself when challenged.

That is the issue. Being unapproachable does not always show up as open hostility. Sometimes it is subtle—silence, distance, avoidance, or passive resistance. But the outcome is the same: the connection breaks down.

Missing Values Of Approachability

When someone is hard to approach, it is easy to assume they are just unfriendly or uninterested. But usually, there is something deeper going on. What is missing is not just a behaviour—**it is a set of values that shape how someone responds to others.**

The First Missing Value Is Humility

Being approachable is not about sounding agreeable or having a soft tone. It comes from a place of humility—the kind that says, "I do not know everything. I am open to learning. I might be wrong, and I am willing to listen."

When someone reacts defensively to feedback or refuses to consider another perspective, it is often because they have tied their self-worth to always being right. They have built their confidence on perfection or control. **The thought of being wrong feels threatening—not just to their pride, but to their identity.**

And when your self-worth is linked to never making mistakes, any form of feedback starts to feel like an attack. A small correction becomes a judgment. A different view becomes a threat. That person is not rejecting you—they are protecting a version of themselves they think they must maintain.

But here is the truth: nobody gets stronger by pushing people away. Growth does not come from defense. It comes from openness.

The Second Missing Value Is Empathy

When someone lacks empathy, they struggle to step outside their own perspective. They do not pause to consider what the other person might be feeling. They do not ask, "Why did they say that?" or "What's going on beneath the words?"

Instead, they assume bad intentions. Honest feedback is labelled as criticism. A moment of honesty is taken as betrayal. Emotional connection gets replaced by misunderstanding.

Empathy shifts that. It helps us hear not just the words, but the emotion behind them. It reminds us that people usually speak up not to attack, but to connect. They want to be understood, to be seen, to feel safe enough to share something important.

Without humility, you cannot listen openly. Without empathy, you cannot understand fully. And when both are missing, people begin to hold back—not because they do not care, but because they no longer feel it is safe to share.

If someone around you hesitates to be honest, or avoids telling you how they really feel, it might not always be because they are unsure of themselves. It might be because they have learned that you do not feel like a safe space for their truth.

Why Do People Become Unapproachable?

Before we assume someone is intentionally shutting others out, it is important to consider what might be happening beneath the surface. Becoming unapproachable is not always a deliberate choice. Many people build emotional walls because they are trying to protect something inside—something they do not know how to express or manage.

Let us take a closer look at what is often behind that wall:

1. Ego and Insecurity: The Mask and the Wound

Some people always want to appear right. They dominate conversations, dismiss ideas, and respond with authority. On the surface, that looks like confidence or control. But underneath, it is usually insecurity.

People who do not feel secure about their own value often try to cover that up with ego. They take control because they are afraid of looking weak. They talk over others because silence makes them uncomfortable. And they reject feedback—not because they are arrogant, but because it feels like exposure.

When someone ties their worth to being right, admitting a mistake feels like failure. So, they close off—even when it means losing real connection.

But the truth is, it takes more strength to admit you are still learning than to pretend you know everything. A person who can say, "I hadn't thought of it that way," shows confidence, not weakness.

2. Fear of Vulnerability: The Fortress That Becomes a Prison

Some people shut down because they have learned, often through painful experiences, that being open leads to being hurt. Maybe they were judged, dismissed, or made to feel foolish for expressing themselves. Maybe someone used their honesty against them.

So, over time, they stopped letting people in. **They replaced vulnerability with control**. They built a version of themselves that looked strong, even if it meant feeling isolated.

But what begins as protection can turn into a trap. They stop getting the very things they want—understanding, connection, support—because people feel pushed away.

Avoiding vulnerability might feel safer, but it often leads to loneliness. And the longer that pattern goes on, the harder it becomes to break.

3. Lack of Emotional Education: Skills We Were Never Taught

Most people were never taught how to handle feedback, manage emotions, or respond with empathy. Schools focus on academics, not emotional intelligence. Families often avoid tough conversations. So, people grow up without learning how to deal with honesty or discomfort.

When someone has never learned how to say, "I hear you," or, "I'm not sure how to respond, but I want to understand," they fall back on avoidance, defensiveness, or shutting down.

It is not because they are unwilling—it is because they have never practiced.

But this is a skill that can be learned. You can become better at receiving feedback. You can learn how to sit with uncomfortable feelings without reacting. And you can create space for people to share without fear.

Emotional openness is not something you are born with. It is something you build through effort and reflection.

And while it is hard to build that openness in ourselves, it can feel even harder when we are reaching out—and someone else will not let us in.

When You Are On the Other Side: Dealing With Someone Unapproachable

Sometimes, you are not the one putting up walls. You are the one trying to reach someone who will not let you in. Maybe it is a partner who shuts down when you express how you feel. Maybe it is a friend who gets defensive whenever you offer feedback. Or maybe it is a colleague or manager who takes every suggestion as a challenge to their authority.

Being in a relationship—whether personal or professional—with someone who is unapproachable is emotionally exhausting. You start editing yourself. You rehearse your words in advance. You avoid bringing up certain topics altogether. And little by little, your voice becomes smaller in the space you share with them.

Over time, this kind of emotional shutdown damages not only the relationship but also your confidence and sense of safety.

So, what can you do?

You may not be able to change the other person, but you can choose how to show up and protect your peace. Here is how:

1. Check Your Approach: Kindness Still Matters

Before assuming someone is completely closed off, take a moment to evaluate your own approach. Ask yourself:

- *Am I coming from a place of care or from frustration?*
- *Am I choosing the right moment to speak?*
- *Am I using a tone that invites conversation or triggers defensiveness?*

This does not mean you are responsible for their behaviour. But approaching with clarity and calm increases the chances of being heard.

2. Express, Then Release: You Cannot Force Change

- You might express yourself clearly and respectfully—and still get no meaningful response. That is not a failure.

- You have done your part. You have spoken with honesty and care.

At that point, it is important to let go of the need for a perfect outcome. People change on their own timeline, not yours. **Sometimes, your words plant a seed that takes time to grow.** Other times, they go unheard.

3. Set Boundaries: You Are Allowed To Step Back

- If the pattern continues—if you keep trying and keep hitting a wall—it is okay to stop pushing.
- You do not have to stay in a one-sided dynamic where your voice is not welcome.

Sometimes, the most respectful thing you can do—for yourself and for the relationship—is to step back and protect your emotional energy.

Why This Matters More Than Ever

In today's world, people speak more than ever, but they do not always connect. **We scroll through posts, react to stories, and attend meetings, but many still feel isolated and unheard.** The emotional space where people can be real with each other is shrinking.

That is why being approachable matters so much now. People want to feel safe in their relationships. They want to be around others who let them speak honestly—without being judged, dismissed, or made to feel like a problem.

You do not have to be the most emotionally skilled person in the room. You just need to be willing to listen, to pause before reacting, and to accept that everyone brings different feelings and experiences. That is what creates a space where people can be themselves.

Being approachable is not about being nice all the time. It is about being real, consistent, and emotionally available.

That day in the hospital taught me something. The doctor did not try to distract me or pretend the fear was not there. She did not give a long speech or act like everything was fine. She just showed up, calm and steady. That alone made all the difference.

So here are a few questions worth asking—not just once, but often:

- Do I make it easy for people to talk to me?

- When someone gives me feedback, do I listen or defend?
- Do I leave space in conversations for others to feel heard?
- Have I ever made someone feel small or shut down when they opened up?
- How can I build more trust in my relationships—at work and at home?

Things To Think About

1. Can you recall a time when someone tried to give you feedback? How did you respond, and what could you have done differently?
2. Think about your close relationships—are there people who hesitate to share things with you? Why might that be?
3. Have you ever kept something to yourself because the other person was not safe to approach? How did that impact the relationship?
4. When was the last time you told someone: "You can always be honest with me"? What might happen if you said it more often?
5. In what areas of your life (work, relationships, family) can you begin practicing more openness and humility starting today?

STAGE 6: FINAL INTEGRATION

(HOLDING BOUNDARIES, CLARITY, AND BALANCE WHILE STAYING CONNECTED TO SELF)

CHAPTER 10

UNDERSTANDING WITHOUT LOSING YOURSELF

We are shaped by more than what we do or say. Every one of us carries the influence of our past—our memories, fears, hopes, and life experiences. From the earliest moments, we begin absorbing how the world treats us. A hug teaches us warmth. A cold glance teaches us to pull away. These everyday moments begin to form how we understand relationships and what we expect from others.

Over time, we start creating internal rules—how people should act, how they should treat us, and how love or respect should look. But the world does not always match those expectations. Each person we meet brings with them a personal history, full of both positive and difficult moments. Their reactions and behaviours are shaped by what they have been through, even if they never talk about it.

Often, what we interpret as rejection or coldness is actually someone's response to something they have not fully processed.

The Invisible Currents – Understanding Human Energy

Have you ever walked into a room and immediately felt at ease with someone—or, on the other hand, felt uncomfortable without knowing why? That is not imagination. It is human energy. Each of us gives off subtle signals shaped by our past experiences, emotions, and environment. You may not see it, but you feel it.

Some people feel open and warm, while others feel distant, even if they are smiling. These patterns often form early. A child raised in a home where affection was freely given might grow up feeling safe and trusting. A child who was often criticized might learn to stay guarded. Someone who felt overlooked might grow up needing to be noticed—not because they are arrogant, but because they fear going unseen.

Our energy shifts depending on what we are going through. Stress, excitement, fear, or disappointment—all of it can change how we come across to others. The more we understand this, the less we expect people to always act a certain way.

The Memorable Trip – When Energy Changed Everything

I was on a road trip from Pune to Goa with three close friends and one woman who was new to our group. It was my first all-girls trip in years, and I could not wait. The first day was full of energy—laughing, singing along to music, and making plans for the days ahead.

But something shifted on the second day. The new girl's attitude toward me changed. She was not openly rude—just cold. She joked with the others, but barely made eye contact with me. Her tone, her body language, her responses—they all felt different. And I could not figure out what had changed.

I kept thinking about our conversations. Did I say something wrong? Did I make her uncomfortable without realizing it? I tried to act normal, but inside, the experience became draining. I was in a beautiful place, surrounded by people, but I felt disconnected and uncomfortable.

Eventually, I realized something important: not all emotional distance is about you. Sometimes it is about the other person. Maybe I reminded her of someone. Maybe she felt out of place and did not know how to connect. **Or maybe she just did not like me. And that is okay.**

Not everyone has to like you. Not every cold reaction needs to be solved. We often put pressure on ourselves to fix what we do not understand. The truth is, **not every connection is meant to stay** in your life. Some people are here to teach us compassion. Some test our patience. Some awaken our self-worth. Others simply pass by to remind us of how far we have come. But **sometimes, the healthier choice is to stop trying to decode every silence—and let go.**

That experience reminded me how easily we mistake other people's moods for personal rejection—when, often, it is something they are carrying that we cannot see.

Everyone Has A Story

Every person is carrying something—an invisible weight that shapes how they speak, react, and move through the world. These invisible backpacks are filled with fears, stress, painful memories, insecurities, and personal struggles. Often, their behaviour has very little to do with us—and everything to do with what they are holding inside.

The cold stranger might be grieving. The cheerful friend might be using smiles to hide their depression. And that colleague who seems distant might be battling with self-doubt or comparing themselves to you—not because you have done something wrong, but because they are wrestling with their own unmet hopes.

It takes maturity to stop assuming every action is about you. It takes inner strength to pause and say, "This may not be personal."

If someone turns cold toward you, you do not need to fight it—or match it. You can observe. You can remain neutral. You can choose silence instead of reaction. You can say to yourself, "This doesn't belong to me."

Your greatest strength is in how you respond. Not with ego, not with defense—but with calm awareness.

Compassion does not mean tolerating everything. It means knowing **when to stay and**

when to step away. When to speak up, and when to protect your peace—without resentment.

So, when someone confuses or hurts you, pause. Ask: *"Is there something going on that I don't know?"* And if you never find the answer, it is still okay to release the weight and walk away a little lighter.

Honouring Yourself While Understanding Others

Understanding others is one of the most compassionate things we can do. It encourages empathy, eases judgment, and opens the door to deeper connection. But there is one truth we often overlook: **you can understand someone deeply without losing yourself in the process.**

Many of us are raised to be kind, to forgive, to offer second chances, and to view the world through empathy. These are powerful values—but without boundaries, they can become exhausting. Especially if you have never been taught how to protect your own emotional well-being in the process.

Empathy does not mean absorbing someone else's pain at your own expense. It does not mean tolerating constant mistreatment or silence, all in the name of "understanding where they are coming from."

Yes, people carry trauma. Yes, they have their own pain. But so do you. And just because their wounds are louder, it does not make yours any less important.

If someone repeatedly makes you feel anxious, invisible, or unsure of yourself, it is okay to pause and ask:

- *Do I feel emotionally safe around this person?*
- *Am I growing here—or slowly shrinking to keep the peace?*

These are not selfish questions. They are essential. These are emotional self-checks that protect your peace and clarity.

We live in a culture that often praises the idea of "fixing" people. We hear stories about sticking by someone through anything and call it strength. But strength is not measured by how much pain you can endure. **Strength also means knowing when to stop compromising your worth. It**

is knowing when to walk away—calmly and without guilt—when the cost becomes too high.

You do not need to burn bridges. You do not need to overexplain your decision or wait for closure. **The moment you decide to choose yourself, that is closure.** You are not meant to keep engaging with people who only notice when you are missing—not when you are there.

Before you move forward, pause and check in: Is there a weight you are carrying that does not belong to you?

Acceptance – The Final Step

Acceptance is not the same as putting up with poor treatment. It is not about building emotional walls either. At its core, acceptance is about choosing peace over the constant need to make sense of other people's behaviour. It is about letting go of the tug-of-war that comes from expecting others to act the way we want them to.

By the time we are asking ourselves, "Why did they do that?" or "Why did they pull away after I showed up for them?" we are already caught in emotional overthinking. That confusion can spiral into self-doubt: "Was it my fault?" But acceptance invites a different question: *"Can I be okay, even if I never know why?"*

The truth is, not every relationship will make sense. Some people will disappear without a clear reason. Some connections will shift quietly, even when you have done everything right. Others will stay in your life—not because they value you, but because it suits them.

In a world where we are always encouraged to react, analyse, or seek closure, acceptance can feel radical. But it is the gentler, stronger choice. It says, "I don't need to know everything to feel okay."

Not every energetic shift needs decoding. Sometimes, the best response is to step back—and protect your own frequency.

You can still understand someone without absorbing their chaos. You can still care deeply—without losing yourself.

Reflection & Closing Practice

Take a quiet moment just for yourself—not as a parent, partner, colleague, or friend—but as the person behind all the roles. Breathe deeply. Allow yourself to pause. Now reflect on the following questions. Let them bring you closer to yourself:

Is there someone in your life whose behaviour still confuses or hurts you?

- What are you hoping they will say or do?
- Could you still find peace if that moment never comes?

Are you holding onto a relationship because of guilt, routine, or fear of letting go?

- What would shift if you gave yourself permission to honour your true feelings?

Can you accept not having all the answers?

- Imagine setting down the need for closure.
- Notice how that feels in your body. Is there ease? Or resistance?

Where in your life are you spending too much energy trying to be understood?

- What would happen if you redirected that energy into understanding yourself?

Now, place your hand gently over your heart. Inhale deeply. Exhale slowly.

Say to yourself, softly and with care:

"I do not need all the answers. I just need peace."

Let that be your anchor—your reminder that not everything requires resolution. Sometimes, simply **choosing yourself over others** is the most powerful step you can take.

FINAL REFLECTION

Beyond The Breaking Point

By the time we reach our breaking point, something inside us has usually been calling out for a long time — quietly, gently, persistently. Not to destroy us. But to awaken us.

This book was not written for perfect people. It was written for the ones who feel stretched thin between chaos and clarity, self and survival, silence, and truth. It was written for those who are tired of shrinking, pleasing, pretending — and ready to return home to themselves.

Each chapter you have just read offered a code. Not a rule, but a reminder.

Not a demand, but a doorway.

You have reflected on what it means to be good — not in the eyes of others, but by your own integrity.

You have explored the cost of silence, the power of truth, and the pain of patterns that repeat until we finally name them.

You have looked closely at your self-worth — not as a byproduct of achievement, but as something deeply rooted and already yours.

You have acknowledged the ache of disappointment in others — and the beauty of still choosing empathy, boundaries, and approachability.

You have learned that healing does not mean never breaking again — it means knowing who you are when you do.

These 10 codes are not just concepts. They are ways of being. Ways of leading — not through control, perfection, or noise, but through presence, clarity, and choice.

You do not need to be loud to be heard.

You do not need to be liked to be valued.

You do not need to be unbreakable to lead.

You just need to start — where you are, with what you have, listening closely to what your inner truth has been trying to tell you all along.

You already have the clarity.

You have just been too distracted to trust it.

If this book reminded you of who you are — even for a moment — then you have already begun your return.

Beyond The Breaking Point is not an end.

It IS THE BEGINNING OF BECOMING.

ACKNOWLEDGMENT

Writing Beyond the Breaking Point has been one of the most humbling and transformative journeys of my life. While the words are mine, the strength behind them has come from the people who have stood beside me, believed in me, and carried me through every high and low.

First and foremost, I express my deepest gratitude to my husband, **Madhur Saini**. Your unwavering commitment, honest feedback, and tireless encouragement helped me stay true to this vision, even when I doubted myself. You never let me give up. You reminded me of my potential when I had forgotten it.

To my mother, **Rupa Kalita**—the very embodiment of selfless service—thank you for your love and quiet strength. To my father, **Sarbeswar Kalita**—who gave me the freedom to become who I truly am—your trust has been my foundation.

To my elder sister **Juli Kalita** and younger sister **Pooja Kalita**—thank you for standing by my side, always cheering for my wildest dreams with unconditional love.

To my brother-in-law **Naba Deka**—thank you for creating space for me to speak and always being there when I needed support.

To my mentors- **Mr. Santosh Singh**—Your steady presence has meant more than words can express. Your kindness, insight, and generosity have helped shape my voice and vision. During one of my difficult phases, when I needed it the most, you helped me see a way forward. Thank you for listening without judgment and offering guidance with a warm heart.

Petra Kupkova—In my most uncertain moments, you showed up with quiet strength—listening with patience and offering feedback that was both kind and clear. Your unwavering support and belief have left a lasting impact on me.

To my dear friends—**Pratham Sehgal**, your help with structuring and refining chapters gave me clarity and direction.

To **David Valles** and **Tulsi Brunda**—Thank you for holding space for my vulnerability, for seeing me at my lowest and never turning away. Your moral support, and unconditional acceptance have been one of the greatest gifts of my life. To **Ashwathy CR**—who stood by me during some of my loneliest and most uncertain days. To **Ambica Desineedi**— for simply being there to listen, I will never forget the comfort of your presence. To **Bharat Dudani**— Every time I shared a piece of good news or a small success with you, your joy felt genuine and boundless.

To all my **readers**—thank you from the bottom of my heart for picking up this book. I hope it speaks to your heart as it did to mine while writing it.

And to my beloved nieces, **Yashika Deka, Diya, and Chia**—your laughter, innocence, and love remind me every day why this world is still so beautiful.

Above all, I bow in gratitude to **God**, for always watching over me, and for sending the right people into my life at the right time. I could not have done this without divine grace.

Thank you, **each and every one of you**, for helping me bring this vision to life.

ABOUT THE AUTHOR

Rimana Dollie K is a lawyer, model, and the reigning Mrs. India Asia 2023 — a rare blend of intellect, elegance, and inner strength. Through every phase of her journey, she has remained rooted in her core values: honesty, empathy, resilience, and clarity.

What sets Dollie apart is not just her success across industries, but her ability to turn personal adversity into a message of healing and transformation. With a background in law and a lifelong commitment to personal growth, she has become a guiding voice for emotional strength, values-based living, and women's empowerment.

A dedicated practitioner of mindfulness and energy awareness, Dollie believes true transformation begins within — by aligning our choices with our deepest truths. Whether navigating professional challenges or emotional chaos, her philosophy is simple: when you return to your values, you return to your power.

Her writing speaks directly to anyone who feels unseen, overwhelmed, or emotionally exhausted. Through practical wisdom and soulful reflection, she offers readers the tools to rediscover their self-worth, reconnect with their purpose, and lead from a place of clarity.

When she is not writing or mentoring, Dollie continues to work as a lawyer, model, and advocate — using every platform to help others live more consciously and courageously.

Follow her ongoing journey of purpose and clarity:

Scan the QR code to connect with her on Instagram.

@RIMANADOLLIEK

RETURN TO SELF - A FRESH BEGINNING

1. What truths have I been avoiding, and what might happen if I finally faced them with compassion?
2. Where in my life have, I stayed silent to keep the peace — and how has that shaped me?
3. Which parts of myself have I neglected, hidden, or denied in order to feel accepted?
4. What recurring patterns in my life are trying to teach me something — and am I ready to listen?
5. What are the values I say I believe in — and do my choices reflect them?
6. Who am I when I am not performing, proving, or pleasing anyone?
7. Where have I confused endurance with strength — and is it time to choose a different skind of power?
8. What does self-worth mean to me when nothing is being achieved, fixed, or validated?

9. Who still has access to me out of guilt, habit, or fear — and what would freedom look like?
10. How do I want to love, lead, and live — now that I've remembered what matters to me?